Recipes With Honey For All Seasons

Diana K. Bricker

Copyright © 2012 Diana K. Bricker

All rights reserved. Do not reproduce or republish in any form, electronic or otherwise, without prior written consent from the author.

ISBN-10: 149539297X
ISBN-13: 978-1495392979

WORDS FROM DIANA

Greetings from the Prairie!

I hope you and your family delight in the Gourmet Country Cuisine featured in this book. It was inspired by my love of cooking and creating recipes as a mother and a professional caterer. It truly gives me joy to feed family, friends, and crowds of people.

I have never retired from food service (even though I have tried). Cooking is not only my life, but my calling. I believe true hospitality is in serving others. Part of my life verse is to "Be inventive in hospitality" from Romans 12:13 (The Message Bible).

A little honey makes everything taste better.

Enjoy!

Diana K. Bricker

TABLE OF CONTENTS

- An Elegant Evening (Chapter 1: Winter) — 1
- Breakfast Buffet Brunch (Chapter 2: Winter) — 11
- Ladies Luncheon (Chapter 3: Spring) — 19
- Celebration Dinner (Chapter 4: Spring) — 28
- Beehive Picnic (Chapter 5: Summer) — 38
- Frontier Barbeque (Chapter 6: Summer) — 46
- Armchair Quarterback Party (Chapter 7: Fall) — 56
- Autumn Harvest (Chapter 8: Fall) — 66
- Honey Tips — 80
- About the Author — 82

Chapter 1: Winter

An Elegant Evening
Welcome your guests with this
up-scale comfort food menu.

- Brie Cheese Smothered in Almonds and Honey
- Fresh French Bread
- Tomato Basil Soup
- Honey Dijon Pork Loin with Cider Gravy
- Oven Roasted Winter Vegetables
- Pear Cranberry Bread Pudding with Honey Caramel Sauce

Brie Cheese Smothered with Almonds and Honey

Here is an easy way to please your guests.

1 round Brie Cheese
½ cup sliced Almonds
½ cup honey

Remove a thin layer off the top of the round of Brie cheese with serrated knife. Place the Brie cheese on a glass dessert plate. Arrange or sprinkle the almonds on the top of the cheese, then drizzle the honey over the almonds. Microwave the dish for 2 minutes. Serve immediately with assorted crackers or warm French bread, and also sliced and green and red apple wedges. Yields 6 servings.

***Tip:** Pecans or any other kind of coarsely chopped nuts may be substituted for the almonds.*

Fresh French Bread

These crusty loaves are great, with or without butter.

½ cup warm water (110 degrees)
2 Tablespoons instant yeast or dry active yeast
2 Tablespoons honey
1½ cups water
1 teaspoon salt
5 cups all-purpose flour
Cornmeal
1 egg
1 Tablespoon of water

Mix the warm water, the yeast and honey in a large bowl. Let rest for 10 minutes or until foamy. Stir in the water and salt. Add the flour, 1 cup at a time, mixing with a wooden spoon until it forms a soft dough. Knead on a lightly floured surface until smooth and elastic, using more flour if needed. Place the dough in a large greased bowl and let rise in a warm place, covered with a damp towel until the dough has doubled (about 1 hour). Punch down the dough and divide it into half. With greased hands, shape each half into long loaves. Grease two baking sheets and then sprinkle them lightly with cornmeal. Place one loaf onto each prepared pan. Make slanted slashes with a sharp knife down each loaf. Cover with plastic wrap. Let the loaves rise for 30 to 45 minutes or until doubled in size. Whisk the egg and tablespoon of water together and brush over the loaves. Bake in a 425 degree oven with a pan of boiling water placed on the bottom rack of the oven for 20 minutes or until the bread sounds hollow when lightly tapped. Cool on a wire rack. Yields 2 large loaves or 4 small ones.

Tip: To make Wheat French Bread, use 3 cups of all-purpose flour and 3 cups of whole wheat flour.

Tomato Basil Soup
This fabulous soup will make tomato lovers
out of anyone!

5 strips bacon diced
½ cup celery, diced
½ cup yellow onion, chopped
½ cup carrot, peeled and shredded
½ cup green bell pepper, diced
½ cup red bell pepper, diced
1 Tablespoon fresh basil, chopped
1 teaspoon fresh garlic, minced
Salt and black pepper to taste
1 Tablespoon honey
2 cups chicken broth
Salt and black pepper to taste
1 - 28 ounce can crushed tomatoes
1 cup heavy cream

Cook the bacon in a medium sized stock pot. Add the celery, onion, carrot, bell peppers, basil, garlic, salt and pepper, honey and the chicken broth. Bring to a boil and simmer for 35 to 45 minutes or until the vegetables are tender. Puree in small batches in the food processor or blender until smooth. Return the puree to the stock pot. Add the crushed tomatoes and simmer for 15 minutes. Add the cream and simmer for 10 minutes, do not boil. Garnish each serving with fresh basil sprigs and diced green bell pepper. Yields 6 first-course servings.

Tip: *For a low fat version, use 1 tablespoon of olive oil for the bacon and skim milk for the cream.*

Honey Dijon Pork Loin with Cider Gravy
This main entree satisfies everyone's taste buds.

1 - 3 to 4 pound boneless pork loin roast
2 Tablespoons Dijon mustard
1 Tablespoon stone ground mustard
1 teaspoon dry mustard
½ cup honey
1 teaspoon garlic, minced
½ teaspoon black pepper

Rinse the pork roast with cool water. Drain on paper towels. Mix 4 the remaining ingredients together and spread onto outside of the pork loin, covering the top and sides. Place onto a rack in a roasting pan. Bake uncovered at 400 degrees for 45 minutes or until the outside of the roast is nicely browned. Cover with the lid or foil. Turn the oven down to 350 degrees and bake for 1- 1½ hours, until the juices run clear. Place on a cutting board and let rest for 10 minutes before slicing. Arrange slices on a serving platter and wrap with foil to keep warm and moist until serving. Serve with the cider gravy. Yields 6 to 8 servings.

Tip: Garnish the serving platter with spiced baby apples or apple slices and fresh rosemary sprigs.

Cider Gravy

Pan drippings and broth from the pork loin roast
1½ cups apple cider
1 - 1 ounce package pork gravy mix
½ cup water

Deglaze the roasting pan with the cider poured into the pan drippings and then heated on the stove in the pan to boiling. Stir with a wooden spoon to scrape and loosen the drippings. Mix the gravy mix and water together in a small mixing bowl, stir into the cider and drippings. Stir constantly until smooth, adding more cider if necessary. Season with salt and pepper to taste. Serve with the pork loin roast. Yields about 2 cups.

Oven Roasted Vegetables
This colorful side dish also is grand
with chicken or beef.

1 butternut squash, peeled and cut into 2-inch pieces
1 pound frozen green beans
2 red onions, quartered
1 pound small red potatoes, cut in half
2 green peppers cut into large chunks
1 pound fresh, small mushrooms
½ cup olive oil
2 teaspoons honey
1 teaspoon rosemary
1 teaspoon sage
2 teaspoons parsley
1 teaspoon minced garlic
Salt and pepper to taste

Place all of the prepared vegetables in a lightly greased roasting or baking pan. Mix the olive oil, honey, rosemary, sage, parsley, garlic, and salt and pepper together in a small mixing bowl until well blended. Pour over the vegetables and toss gently with a wooden spoon or your hands. Bake uncovered at 350 degrees for 1 to 1½ hours or until the vegetables test done with a fork. Yields 6 side dish servings.

Tip: Make a great veggie soup with the leftovers by chopping up the vegetables; and then heating with chicken or beef stock and canned tomatoes.

Pear-Cranberry Bread Pudding With Honey Caramel Sauce

Place each serving in pretty dessert dishes with the sauce drizzled on top.

8 cups leftover cinnamon rolls or sweet bread, torn into chunks
4 eggs
2 cups half and half
½ cup honey
1 teaspoon cinnamon
½ teaspoon nutmeg
1 teaspoon vanilla
2 fresh pears, peeled and chopped
1 cup dried cranberries

Mix all ingredients in a large bowl, adding more half-and-half if the mixture seems dry. The bread mixture should be very moist. Place into a greased 4 quart casserole dish. Bake the bread pudding, uncovered at 350 degrees for 45 minutes or until a knife inserted into the center comes out clean. Keep warm until serving time and serve with the Honey Caramel Sauce. Yields 8 large or 12 small servings.

Honey Caramel Sauce
½ cup butter
1½ cups brown sugar
½ cup honey
1 cup heavy cream
1 teaspoon vanilla

Melt the butter, brown sugar, honey and cream together in a medium saucepan, stirring to blend well. Bring to a boil and boil gently for 2 minutes. Stir in the vanilla and keep warm until serving time. Yields about 2 cups.

Tip: *Serve this yummy sauce over ice cream, pound cake or brownies.*

Chapter 2: More Winter

Breakfast Buffet Brunch
This menu works well on a busy holiday morning. Almost everything can be made up the night before.

- Blueberry Scones
- Apple-Croissant Brunch Bake
- Sweet Potato Biscuits
- Honey Glazed Ham
- Lemon Cream Cheese Danishes
- Spiced Honey Tea

Blueberry Scones
These flaky, tender treats will melt in your mouth.

3 cups all-purpose flour
2½ teaspoons baking powder
½ teaspoon salt
¾ cup butter
1 cup fresh or dried blueberries
1 cup buttermilk
1/3 cup honey

Combine the flour, baking powder and salt in a medium-mixing bowl. Cut in the butter with a pastry blender until mixture is crumbly. Add the blueberries, tossing gently. Mix the buttermilk and honey with a whisk in a small bowl. Stir the buttermilk mixture into the blueberry-flour mixture, carefully. Turn out to a board with plenty of flour and knead gently 4 to 5 times. Pat the dough into a 10-inch circle on a lightly greased baking sheet. Brush with the glaze. Cut into 12 wedges, separate slightly. Bake at 400 degrees for 20 to 25 minutes or until the scones are lightly browned. Serve warm. Yields 1 dozen scones.

Glaze:

¼ cup whipping cream
1 to 2 Tablespoons of honey

Mix the cream and honey together in a small mixing bowl. Brush over scones before cutting and baking.

Tip: Coat the fresh blueberries in a little flour before adding them to the dry ingredients. Other chopped dried fruit may be used for the blueberries.

Apple-Croissant Brunch Bake

This do- ahead dish is great served with bacon or sausage links.

6 croissants, sliced
8 large eggs
1 cup milk
1 teaspoon vanilla
1 teaspoon cinnamon
½ teaspoon nutmeg
¼ cup honey
2 Granny Smith Apples, cored and thinly sliced
Cinnamon and sugar to sprinkle over the apples
1/3 cup butter

Grease a 9 x 13-inch baking pan and layer the sliced croissants into the pan. Blend the eggs, milk, vanilla, cinnamon, nutmeg, and honey until smooth. Pour over the croissants. Cover with plastic wrap and chill overnight or for at least 4 hours. Uncover and lay the apple slices in rows over the croissant mixture. Sprinkle the apple slices with cinnamon and sugar, then dot the butter over the top. Bake at 350 degrees for 50 minutes or until the eggs are set and the apples are done when tested with a fork. Let the casserole set for 10 minutes before serving. Cut into 12 squares. Serve with extra honey or maple syrup.

***Tip:** To interchange this dish, use fresh or canned, drained peaches or pears for the apples.*

Sweet Potato Biscuits
Always a great addition to any lunch or dinner.

2 cups flour
3 teaspoons baking powder
1 teaspoon salt
1/3 cup shortening
1 cup mashed sweet potatoes
¼ cup honey
½ cup heavy cream
Enough milk to moisten

Sift the flour, baking powder, and salt into a medium mixing bowl. Cut in the shortening with a pastry blender until crumbly. Stir in the mashed sweet potatoes, honey, and cream until blended. Add enough milk to moisten, but do not make the dough too sticky.
Turn out onto a lightly floured board and pat out thickly. Cut into circles with a biscuit cutter and place on a lightly greased baking sheet. Bake at 425 degrees for 10 to 12 minutes or until biscuits are lightly browned. Serve piping hot. Yields 1 dozen.

Tip: *To make your biscuits rise higher when baking, place biscuits next to each other on the baking sheet before baking.*

Honey Glazed Ham

Make this the day before, slice the ham thinly,
warm in the oven, tightly covered
in an oven-safe serving dish.

1 - 4 to 5 pound boneless, teardrop or fully cooked ham
1 cup brown sugar
½ cup honey
1 teaspoon dry ground mustard
½ cup apricot preserves

Place the ham into a shallow roasting pan, cut side down. Mix the brown sugar, honey, dry mustard, and apricot preserves into a small saucepan. Bring to a boil. Baste the ham with the sugar-honey glaze. Bake at 350 degrees for 1 to 1½ hours, basting the ham with the glaze every 15 minutes. When the ham is done, baste and place under the broiler for about 2 to 3 minutes to get a nicely browned coating. Let the ham set for 10 minutes for ease in slicing. Slice thick or tl1in and pile onto a serving platter. Serve hot. Yields 12 or more servings.

Tip: *A bone-in-ham would also work. Bake at 325 degrees for or about 2 to 2½ hours.*

Lemon Cream Cheese Danishes
These simple, finger-shaped pastries will make your guests think that you slaved for hours.

1 Tablespoon dry yeast
½ cup lukewarm water
1 teaspoon honey
1 egg, slightly beaten
2 cups flour
½ teaspoon salt
¾ cup butter-flavored shortening
16 ounces cream cheese, softened
½ cup sugar
½ cup honey
1 teaspoon lemon juice
½ teaspoon lemon rind
Glaze

Combine the first 3 ingredients in a small mixing bowl and let set until bubbly. Add the egg and mix well. In a medium-mixing bowl sift the flour and salt together. Cut in the shortening until crumbly. Add the yeast mixture and mix well. Knead on a floured board until smooth. Roll out into a large rectangle. Combine the cream cheese, sugar, honey, lemon juice, and lemon rind until smooth. Spread the cream cheese mixture onto the middle of the dough, Take one side of the longest part of the dough and fold over the filling. Fold the other side of the dough on top. Fold the ends up 1½ inches and pinch closed. Place onto a lightly greased baking sheet or jellyroll pan.Bake at 375 degrees for 25 minutes or until lightly browned. Let cool completely before drizzling the glaze, over the top. Cut into 12 long, finger-shaped slices. Yields 1 dozen.

Glaze:

1 cup powdered sugar, sifted
1 teaspoon lemon juice
1 Tablespoon cream
2 Tablespoons honey

Whisk all ingredients together until smooth. Yields 1/3 cup of glaze.

Tip: *Use vanilla for the lemon juice; omit lemon rind in the filling for the Danish; then use vanilla instead of lemon juice for the glaze.*

Spiced Honey Tea
Have your tea drinkers add more honey
to their own cups, if desired.

8 cups water
1 cup honey
1 orange, cut into thin wedges
2 sticks cinnamon
Pinch nutmeg
8 of your favorite blend of black or herbal tea bags

Mix the water and honey together in a medium sauce pan or tea-pot. Add the orange wedges and spices. Bring to a full boil. Turn off the heat and add the tea bags. Cover and let steep for 2 minutes. Strain into a serving carafe or tea pot. Serve hot. Yields 8 cups of tea.

Tip: *Use lemon or orange flavored tea bags to add more zest. Garnish each teacup with a lemon or orange wedge.*

Chapter 3: Spring

Ladies Luncheon
A bridal shower or a neighborhood get together
set the perfect stage for this showcase
of women-friendly food.

- Spicy Peanut Chicken and Pasta
- Layered Vegetable Salad
- Vinaigrette Dressing
- Carrot and Pineapple Muffins
- Honey Citrus Cheesecake with Berry Puree
- Sparkling Pink Lemonade

Spicy Peanut Chicken and Pasta
A taste of the Orient that will delight your guests.

1 teaspoon Chinese 5-spice powder
1 teaspoon garlic, minced
1 teaspoon curry powder
1 teaspoon cayenne pepper
1 teaspoon ginger
1/3 cup honey
2 Tablespoons soy sauce
1 Tablespoon sherry or vinegar
¼ cup creamy peanut butter
¼ cup sesame or vegetable oil, plus 2 tablespoons
6 - 4 ounce boneless, skinless chicken breasts
1 red bell pepper, cut into thin strips
1 yellow bell pepper, cut into thin strips
½ cup green onion, sliced
12 ounces vermicelli noodles, cooked al dente and cooled
1 cup salted peanuts

Mix the spices with the honey, soy sauce, sherry, peanut butter and the ¼ cup of oil with a wire whisk in a small bowl until smooth. Place the chicken breasts in a re-sealable plastic bag and pour one-half of the honey-spice mixture over the chicken. Place the cooked noodles in another bag and pour the other half of the marinade over the noodles and seal. Chill the chicken and noodles for 3 hours or overnight. Remove the chicken from the marinade and discard marinade. Grill or broil the chicken for 6 to 9 minutes on each side or until the chicken is no longer pink. Place in a baking dish and cover with foil and keep warm in a 250-degree oven until serving time. Stir-fry the bell peppers and green onion in a skillet with the 2 tablespoons of oil for 2 to 3 minutes on high or until tender-crisp. Add the vermicelli noodles with the marinade and peanuts. Stir-fry for 3 to 5 minutes or until the noodles are warm. Place 1½ to 2 cups of the stir-fry mixture on each individual serving plate. Cut each cooked chicken breast into l-inch slices and place on the noodle mixture. Serve hot. Yields 6 servings.

Tip: Garnish with pepper rings and green onions.

Layered Vegetable Salad
This can also be layered on individual plates.

3 cups fresh baby spinach leaves, divided
1 cup red radish slices
1 medium cucumber, sliced
1 cup fresh mushrooms, sliced
1 small red onion, sliced
1 cup frozen peas, thawed slightly
1- 8 ounce can of water chestnuts, sliced

Layer one half of the spinach leaves in the bottom of a trifle dish or large clear glass bowl. Add the radishes, cucumber, and fresh mushrooms in layers. Lay the remaining spinach over the mushrooms and add the red onion, frozen peas, and the water chestnuts in layers. Chill covered with plastic wrap until serving time. Serve with the following vinaigrette dressing or your favorite salad dressing.

Tip: *If you do not have a bowl that is suitable, use a glass 9 x 13-inch baking dish*

Vinaigrette Dressing

This tangy dressing was a favorite of my catering clients.

2/3 cup olive oil
1/3 cup red wine vinegar
1/3 cup honey
1 teaspoon salt
1 teaspoon black pepper
1 teaspoon Spice Islands Salad Seasoning for Vinaigrette

Mix all together in a jar with a tight fitting lid. Store and serve at room temperature. Yields 1 1/3 cups of dressing.

Tip: *Raspberry vinegar is another flavor that adds pizzazz to this dressing.*

Carrot and Pineapple Muffins

Bake these in mini-muffin cups so each guest can have more than one.

2 cups flour
1½ teaspoons cinnamon
1 teaspoon baking powder
½ teaspoon baking soda
½ teaspoon salt
2 eggs
1 cup sour cream '
¼ cup butter, melted
1 cup honey
½ cup grated carrot
½ cup crushed pineapple, well drained

Sift dry ingredients together in a small mixing bowl, set aside. In a medium bowl, mix the eggs, sour cream, melted butter, and honey together with a whisk until smooth. Stir in the carrots and pineapple. Add the dry ingredients, stirring until just moistened. Spoon into paper lined or greased regular muffin tins, filling them 2/3's full. Bake at 400 degrees for 20 to 25 minutes or until golden brown. Yields 18 regular-sized muffins, 36 mini-muffins or 12 Texas-sized muffins.

Tip: Serve these with honey butter: mix ½ cup of softened butter with 2 tablespoons of hone with a fork. Yields ½ cup.

Honey Citrus Cheesecake with Berry Puree
This no bake dessert makes a grand finale
for any special occasion.

1 envelope unflavored gelatin
½ cup lime juice
½ cup sugar
½ cup honey
2 large eggs, beaten
16 oz. Cream cheese, softened
1 teaspoon orange zest
1 teaspoon lemon zest
2 cups whipping cream
2 cups key lime or lemon flavored sandwich cookie crumbs
1/3 cup melted butter

Dissolve the gelatin in the lime juice in a medium saucepan. Let set for 5 minutes. Add sugar, honey, and eggs, whisking until smooth. Cook over medium heat, stirring constantly until thickened, about 3 to 5 minutes. Remove from heat and let cool. Whip the cream cheese until light and fluffy. Add the orange and lemon zests. Gradually add the lime mixture, beating until smooth. Cover and chill for 25 minutes. Whip the cream until stiff. Fold into the lime cream cheese mixture. Cover and chill for 15 minutes. Mix the cookie crumbs and melted butter together and press into a 9-inch spring-form pan. Gently spoon in the lime cheesecake mixture. Cover with plastic wrap and chill for 3 to 4 hours or until set. Unmold and place on a cake plate. Serve with the Berry Puree. Cut into 12 wedges.

Tip: Garnish with drained mandarin oranges, lime and lemon twists.

Berry Puree:

1- 12 ounce package frozen berry mix: blueberries, strawberries, raspberries, thawed
1 cup honey
2 Tablespoons orange juice

Puree all ingredients in the food processor or blender until smooth. Spoon about 1/3 cup of the puree onto each serving plate. Set the cheesecake slice in the center and garnish.

Tip: Serve leftover puree on vanilla ice cream or angel food cake with whipped cream.

Sparkling Pink Lemonade

This non-alcoholic beverage is perfect for ladies of all ages.

2 quarts pink lemonade made from a pre-packaged mix
¼ cup strawberry syrup
¼ cup honey
1 liter ginger ale, chilled
Ice
1 pint of fresh strawberries, cleaned

Mix the lemonade, strawberry syrup and honey together and chill. Fill each beverage glass half full of ice. Place a strawberry in each glass. Pour the lemonade over the ice and fruit, filling 2/3 full. Fill to the rim with the ginger ale. Yields 12 or more servings.

Tip: Lemons may also be used as a garnish. For ease in serving, fill a large punchbowl with the lemonade mixture and an ice ring made of frozen strawberries and lemon slices. Add the ginger ale just before serving.

Chapter 4: Spring

Celebration Dinner
Use this Mediterranean themed menu to honor a graduate or birthday.

- Marinated Greek Salad with Honey-Dill Dressing
- Lamb and Vegetable Kabobs
- New Potatoes Au Gratin
- Honey Glazed Baby Carrots
- Almond Braided Bread
- Fresh Fruit Tray with a Lemon Yogurt Honey Crème

Marinated Greek Salad
with Honey-Dill Dressing

The marinated vegetables may also be served alone as a buffet side dish.

Vegetables to marinate in dressing:

1 pound fresh green beans, snapped and cooked tender crisp, about 10 minutes
1 red onion, halved and sliced
1 cup ripe olives, cut into halves
2 large tomatoes cut into wedges
1 cucumber, sliced

Honey Dill Dressing:

¾ cup olive oil
1/3 cup red wine vinegar
¼ cup honey
1 teaspoon garlic
2 teaspoons dill weed
1 Tablespoon lemon juice
Salt and pepper to taste

6 cups fresh salad greens
1 cup Tomato-Basil flavored Feta cheese, crumbled

Place the vegetables in a large glass or plastic bowl. Shake up the dressing ingredients in a jar with a tight fitting lid or blend for about 2 minutes in the blender. Pour the dressing over the vegetables and toss gently. Chill, covered overnight or for at least 4 hours to allow the flavors to blend. Arrange about 1 cup of fresh greens on a chilled salad plate. Spoon a serving of the marinated veggies onto the greens. Top the veggies with a small amount of the Feta cheese. Yields 6 to 8 servings.

Tip: *Used canned or frozen beans for the fresh green beans.*

Lamb and Vegetable Kabobs
Nothing is tastier than tender, lean, farm raised lamb!

2 pounds lamb tenderloin or boneless lamb chops, cut into 1 to 2-inch cubes

Marinade:
½ cup brown sugar
½ cup honey
½ cup olive or vegetable oil
¼ cup soy sauce
¼ cup sherry or red wine vinegar
1 teaspoon garlic
1 teaspoon basil
1 teaspoon oregano
Salt and pepper to taste

4 cups of any combination of the following vegetables:
Red or yellow onions cut into large chunks
Red, green, yellow or orange bell peppers cut into large chunks
Eggplant, cut into 1-inch chunks
Small zucchini, sliced into 2-inch slices
Whole fresh mushrooms
Olive oil for brushing

Mix the marinade ingredients together and pour over the lamb cubes which have been placed in a plastic bag. Seal bag and chill overnight. Discard marinade. Place lamb cubes, alternating with the vegetables on skewers. Brush the olive oil over the vegetables.

Grill on high heat, turning frequently, until evenly browned and the meat is done. Yields 12 kabobs.

Tip: *This also is delicious with beef, pork or chicken.*

New Potatoes Au Gratin

2 ½ pounds new red potatoes
½ cup butter
1/3 cup flour
2 cups cream
2 teaspoons honey
1 clove garlic, minced
Salt and pepper to taste
¼ teaspoon nutmeg
2 cups shredded Romano cheese
½ cup parsley

Slice the new potatoes and place in a large bowl. Cover with ice water. Melt the butter in a medium saucepan. Whisk in the flour, stirring until smooth. Add the cream, honey, garlic, salt, pepper, and nutmeg. Cook over low heat, whisking until smooth and thickened (about 3 minutes). Drain the potatoes and pat dry on paper towels. Layer ½ of the potatoes in a buttered casserole dish. Pour ½ of the cream sauce over the potatoes. Sprinkle 1 cup of the cheese over cream sauce. Sprinkle with parsley. Repeat layers. Bake covered for 30 minutes at 375 degrees. Uncover and finish baking for 30 to 40 more minutes or until potatoes are done when pricked with a fork, and the top is nicely browned. Yields 6 to 8 servings.

Tip: Garnish with additional Romano Cheese and fresh parsley.

Honey Glazed Baby Carrots
This is a favorite of my sons, nieces and grandkids.

2 cups water
1 chicken flavored bouillon cube
2 pounds baby carrots
¼ cup butter
½ cup honey

Dissolve the bouillon cube in the water in a large saucepan. Add the carrots. Bring to a boil and cook for 20 to 30 minutes or until the carrots are tender. Drain and return to pan. Melt the butter and honey together in a small glass bowl or 2 cup glass measuring cup in the microwave for 2 minutes. Pour over the cooked carrots. Gently stir and keep warm on low heat until serving time. Yields 6 servings.

Tip: *Carrots julienned or cut into slices may be used for the baby carrots.*

Almond Braided Bread

This amazing bread that will make any event special.
It is well worth the effort.

2 packages dry yeast
¾ cup warm water
1 teaspoon honey
½ cup milk
4 eggs
½ cup melted butter
¾ cup honey
1 teaspoon salt
2 teaspoons orange zest
2 teaspoons lemon zest
½ cup almonds, chopped
6 cups flour

Dissolve the yeast with the warm water and 1 teaspoon of honey. Let rest for 5 minutes. Mixture should be bubbly. Mix the milk, eggs, butter, ½ cup of honey, salt, orange and lemon zest together in a large mixing bowl. Add the yeast mixture. Mix until smooth,
Then add 3 cups of the flour, beating until smooth. Mix in the remaining flour one cup at a time, until it forms a ball. Then fold in the chopped almonds. Knead on a lightly floured board until smooth and elastic. Place in a well-oiled large bowl. Cover with a damp towel and let raise in a warm place so for 1 hour or until doubled. Punch down dough. Divide dough in half. Then divide each half into thirds and roll each into long ropes. Grease 2 baking sheets. Place 3 ropes in the center of each pan. Starting at one end, braid the ropes loosely together and turn the ends under the braid. Repeat with the other pan. Cover each pan with plastic wrap and let raise until doubled in a warm place for

about 20 to 30 minutes. Bake at 350 degrees for 45 to 50 minutes or until the loaves sound hollow when lightly tapped and are nicely browned. Brush hot loaves with butter for a soft crust. Yields 2 large loaves.

Tip: *To make a heartier loaf of bread, use 3 cups of whole wheat flour for 3 cups of the white flour.*

Fruit Tray with Lemon Honey Yogurt Crème

Served alone or with other desserts,
this makes a marvelous addition to any festivity.

Assorted fresh fruits;
Melons, cut into wedges or made into cubes or balls
Grapes, red, green and purple, snipped into small clusters
Oranges, cut into wedges
Strawberries, cleaned with the stems on for color
Apricots, fresh and peeled or dried

Arrange on a large platter or tray, alternating colors. Chill until serving time. Serve with the crème for dipping.

Tip: *Cut the fruit into bit-sized pieces and place in individual dishes. Top with the crème.*

Lemon Honey Yogurt Crème

1- 8 ounce package cream cheese
1- 8 ounce container lemon yogurt
1 teaspoon lemon zest
1 teaspoon lemon juice
½ cup honey

Blend all ingredients together in mixer or food processor until smooth. Place into a small serving bowl and cover until ready to serve. Yields 1½ cups of yogurt crème.

Tip: *Use orange or vanilla-flavored yogurt for the lemon flavor.*

Chapter 5: Summer

Beehive Picnic

Get out the basket and blanket to enjoy this lunchtime feast by the lake or right out-doors in your own back yard.

- Cucumber Tomato Red Onion Salad
- Veggie Pasta Salad
- Honey Glazed Fruit Salad
- Honey Mustard Chicken Salad Wraps
- White Chocolate - Macadamia Nut Brownies
- Peach Honey Tea

Cucumber Tomato Red Onion Salad

This salad is better if made the day before to allow the flavors to blend.

3 large cucumbers, sliced
3 ripe tomatoes cut into wedges
1 medium red onion, cut in half and sliced

Dressing:
⅔ cup vegetable oil
⅓ cup raspberry flavored vinegar
⅓ cup fresh orange juice
⅔ cups honey
2 teaspoons salt and black pepper

Place the vegetables in a medium bowl. Shake up dressing ingredients in a jar with a tight fitting lid. Pour over the vegetables. Cover and chill. Gently toss the salad before serving. Yields 6 servings.

Tip: *The dressing is also great on a tossed green salad.*

Veggie Pasta Salad

This was one of our standard pasta salads
which we served to catering customers.

1- 12 ounce package tri-colored Rotini pasta, cooked al dente and drained
½ cup yellow onion, diced
½ cup carrot, shredded or chopped
½ cup celery, diced
1½ cups *Miracle Whip Salad Dressing*
1 teaspoon prepared yellow mustard
2 teaspoons cider vinegar
¼ cup honey
1 teaspoon seasoning salt
1 teaspoon black pepper
1 teaspoon celery salt

Mix the pasta, onion, carrot, and celery in a medium mixing bowl. Mix the Miracle Whip, mustard, vinegar, honey, seasoning salt, black pepper, and celery salt. Mix with the pasta and veggies, stirring to blend well, Cover and chill until serving time. Yields 6 to 8 servings.

Tip: *Try another cooked pasta such as shells, penne or macaroni.*

Honey Glazed Fruit Salad

The natural juices in the fresh fruits mix with
the glaze to make this an ideal summertime salad.

⅓ cup honey
⅓ cup frozen orange juice, undiluted
4 cups of assorted fresh fruits such as:
Pineapple, cut into chunks
Melons, chunks or made into balls
Red or green grapes
Strawberries, stemmed and sliced

Heat the honey and orange juice in the microwave in a glass measuring cup for 2 minutes. Gently mix the fruit in a large bowl. Pour the glaze over the fruit and toss gently. Cover and chill until serving time. Yields 6 to 8 servings.

Tip: Use any other frozen orange blend fruit juice mix such as Orange-Mango-Peach to add more flavor.

Honey Mustard Chicken Salad Wraps

These colorful wraps make a great addition to any picnic.
The sprouts make great sandwich fillers;
they stay crisp when packed ahead of time.

Salad:
4 cups cooked, diced chicken
1 cup celery, diced
½ cup onion, chopped
1½ cups Mayo
1 teaspoon Dijon mustard
⅓ cup honey
1 teaspoon dry mustard
1 teaspoon curry powder
1 teaspoon garlic salt
1 teaspoon black pepper
1 teaspoon paprika

Wrap makings:
2 cups fresh alfalfa sprouts
2 avocados, peeled and sliced
1 cup cheddar cheese, shredded
6 tomato or spinach flavored tortillas

Mix the chicken, celery, onion, Mayo, mustards, honey, curry powder, garlic salt, pepper, and paprika in a medium mixing bowl. Cover and chill for 2 hours. Assemble the wraps in the following manner: place ¾ cup of the chicken salad in the center of 1 wrap. Sprinkle a ¼ cup of the sprouts over the chicken salad. Lay 3 to 4 slices of the avocados on the sprouts lengthwise. Sprinkle the shredded cheese over the avocados. Wrap the tortillas burrito-style covering the filling with the ends, then folding the sides over the ends. Wrap each sandwich with plastic or parchment paper until serving time. Cut diagonally in the center of each wrap just before serving. Yields 6 servings.

Tip: *To please picky palettes serve all of the sandwich makings in separate bowls and have each person make his or her own sandwiches.*

Honey White Chocolate - Macadamia Nut Brownies

Cut these into small bite-sized pieces
to make them into fun finger food.

1 cup butter, melted
1 cup brown sugar
¾ cup honey
2 teaspoons vanilla
4 eggs
¾ cup cocoa powder
1 cup flour
½ teaspoon baking powder
½ teaspoon baking soda
¼ teaspoon salt
1 cup macadamia nuts, chopped
1 cup white chocolate morsels

Mix the butter, sugar, honey, and vanilla together in a medium mixing bowl. Add the eggs, one at a time until well mixed. Mix the dry ingredients together and add to the egg and sugar mixture. Blend well. Pour the batter into a greased 9 x 13-inch pan. Sprinkle the nuts and morsels over the batter. Bake at 350 degrees for 30 or 35 minutes. Do not over-bake. Let cool, then cut into small squares. Yields 24 bars.

Tip: *Spread the top of the cooled brownies with your favorite chocolate frosting for extra decadence. Store the brownies in an airtight container to keep them moist.*

Honey Peach Tea

Cool off from the heat with this refreshingly sweet drink.

3 quarts boiling water
8 regular tea bags
1 cup honey
1 cup peach nectar
1 cup frozen peach slices
Ice

Steep the tea bags in the boiling water for 5 minutes. Remove the tea bags. Pour the tea into a large gallon pitcher or jar. Heat the honey and peach nectar together until blended in a saucepan, about 2 minutes. Pour the honey-peach mixture into the tea. Let cool to room temperature, Add the frozen peach slices. Chill the tea until serving time. Serve in ice-filled glasses. Yields 1 gallon of honey-peach tea.

Tip: Make this Honey-Peach-Suntea by placing 3 quarts of water and the tea bags into a gallon jar with a tight fitting lid. Set out in the sun for 3 to 4 hours. Remove the tea bags than add the honey peach mixture and frozen peaches. Chill before serving.

Chapter 6: Summer

Frontier Barbecue
Serve this Western-style with red handkerchiefs as napkins and serve your favorite beverages out of mason jars.

- Country-Style BBQ Ribs
- Calico Baked Beans
- Great Plains Potato Salad
- Ice Box Coleslaw
- Old-Fashioned Corn Bread
- Double Berry Pie with Honeyed Whipped Cream

Country-Style BBQ Ribs

A first choice main dish for the Fourth of July or family reunions. We like to eat ours de-boned and then avoid the mess, by using a fork.

6 to 8 pounds country-style boneless pork ribs
Garlic salt, black pepper and chili powder to taste

Sprinkle the ribs with the spices and place on a baking rack. Bake in a 325 degree oven for 1 to 1½ hours or until browned. Drain and grill the ribs basting with the BBQ sauce frequently, grilling for 30 to 45 minutes or until the ribs are done. Serve with additional sauce. Yields 12 servings.

BBQ Sauce:
4 cups ketchup
½ cup brown sugar
½ cup honey
½ cup molasses
2 Tablespoons prepared yellow mustard
1 Tablespoon Worcestershire sauce
1 teaspoon Tabasco sauce
1 teaspoon garlic salt
1 Tablespoon black pepper
⅓ cup chili powder
1 teaspoon cayenne pepper
¼ cup dried onion flakes or ½ cup minced onion

Mix all the sauce ingredients into a large stock-pot or crock-pot. Simmer for 4 to 5 hours. Yields ½ gallon of sauce. Store the remaining sauce in an airtight container in the refrigerator.

Tip: *Because of our ever-changing weather in South Dakota, I finish cooking the ribs in an electric roaster oven or large crock-pot when the wind or rain makes grilling impossible. Place the ribs in the bottom of the roaster, then cover them thoroughly with the BBQ sauce and bake and baste them for 2 or more hours at 325 degrees or until the ribs are done. They can also be finished in the oven at 325 degrees, basting with sauce.*

Calico Baked Beans

A South Dakota BBQ wouldn't be complete without beans, a Western staple in the early days on the frontier.

1- 30 ounce can pork and beans, undrained
1- 15 ounce can pinto beans, drained
1- 15 ounce can butter beans, drained
1- 15 ounce can red kidney beans, drained
1- 15 ounce cans black beans, drained
1 large onion, chopped
½ pound bacon, chopped and cooked until crisp
1 cup ketchup
½ cup honey
½ cup molasses
¼ cup brown sugar
2 Tablespoons prepared yellow mustard

Place all the ingredients into a 3 quart baking dish, stirring to mix well. Bake at 325 degrees for 2 to 3 hours, uncovered. Serve warm. Yields 10 to 12 servings.

Tip: *Make this your crock-pot to keep the kitchen cool.*

Great Plains Potato Salad

At our house we prefer this picnic favorite
a little dry and strong on the mustard. Add more salad
dressing and less mustard to suit your own taste.

5 pounds red potatoes, boiled with skins on and cooled to room temperature
6 hard boiled eggs, chopped
1 large onion, chopped
1 cup dill pickle, chopped
½ cup vinegar and oil dressing
2 cups Miracle Whip Salad Dressing
3 Tablespoons prepared yellow mustard
2 teaspoons honey
1 teaspoon Worcestershire sauce
Season to taste: salt, black pepper garlic and paprika

Peel the cooled potatoes and dice into a large mixing bowl. Pour the vinegar and oil dressing over the potatoes. Add the eggs, onion, and pickle. Mix the remaining ingredients together in a small mixing bowl. Pour over the potato mixture and blend well. Place into a serving bowl, cover and chill until serving time. Yields 12 servings.

Tip: When in a hurry, peel and dice the potatoes before boiling. Cook at a slow boil until just tender, about 20 minutes, then drain. Follow the remaining directions. Garnish with sliced, hard cooked eggs, paprika and dill pickles.

Ice Box Coleslaw

This is a family recipe that is a wonderful addition to any summertime meal; it travels well to potlucks, there isn't any mayonnaise to worry about setting out too long in the heat.

1 head green cabbage, coarsely shredded
½ cup purple cabbage, coarsely shredded
1 cup red, green or yellow bell pepper, diced
1 small yellow onion, chopped

Place into a medium plastic or glass mixing bowl. Pour the hot dressing over the cabbage mixture. Stir after the mixture has cooled to room temperature. Place in a serving bowl and cover tightly. Chill until serving time. Stir before serving.

Dressing:
⅔ cup honey
3 Tablespoons salt
⅔ cup vegetable oil
1 cup white vinegar

Bring all the ingredients to a boil in a saucepan. Boil for 2 to 3 minutes.

Tip: *This salad will keep for up to 2 weeks in the refrigerator. Garnish with bell pepper rings.*

Old-Fashioned Corn Bread
Golden quick bread smothered with honey makes it almost unnecessary to have dessert.

2 cups yellow cornmeal
2 cups flour
2 Tablespoons baking powder
½ teaspoon baking soda
2 teaspoons salt
½ cup honey
2 cups buttermilk
4 eggs
4 Tablespoons bacon grease drippings or melted butter

Mix the cornmeal, four, baking powder, baking soda, and salt it together in a medium mixing bowl. Add the honey, buttermilk, eggs and 2 tablespoons of the bacon drippings or butter and stir until just moistened. Pour batter into a 9 x 13-inch baking pan or two 9-inch pie pans, Drizzle the remaining 2 tablespoons of bacon drippings or melted butter over the top of the batter. Bake at 400 degrees for 20 minutes or until a pick comes out clean. Cut into 12 squares. Serve hot with butter and honey. Yields 12 servings.

Tip: *Add a 15 ounce can of whole kernel corn, (drained) to the batter to make it double corn bread.*

Double Berry Pie with Honeyed Whipped Cream

Commemorate any patriotic holiday with this
red, white, and blue scrumptious ending.

1 - 9-inch baked pastry shell, in a pie or tart pan
2 cups strawberries, washed, drained and the stems removed
1 cup blueberries, washed and drained
1 cup honey
1½ cups water
2 Tablespoons of cornstarch
1- 3 ounce box of strawberry flavored gelatin

Arrange the berries into the baked pie shell. Mix the honey, water, and cornstarch until smooth in a medium-saucepan. Bring to a boil and boil for 2 minutes, stirring constantly until thick. Add the strawberry gelatin and stir until dissolved. Let cool for 10 minutes. Then spoon over the berries in the pie shell. Chill for 3 hours or until firm. Serve with the whipped cream. Yields 1 pie or 8 servings.

Honeyed Whipped Cream

2 cups heavy whipping cream, well chilled
¼ cup honey
½ of a 3-ounce box of French Vanilla pudding mix

Mix all of the ingredients together in a large mixing bowl and whip until cream is stiff and peaks form when the beater is lifted out. Serve on the Double Berry Pie. Yields 2 cups of whipped cream.

Tip: *Add raspberries of blackberries with the strawberries to make a triple berry pie.*

RECIPES WITH HONEY FOR ALL SEASONS

Chapter 7: Fall

Armchair Quarterback Party
A perfect menu for a Sunday autumn afternoon, while calling out the plays for your favorite team.

- Honey Ranch Dip with Veggie Tray
- Sweet and Tangy Meatballs
- Mini Pigs in Blankets with Honey Mustard Sauce
- Honey BBQ Glazed Chicken Wings
- Apples with Honey Caramel Cinnamon Dip
- Honey Nut Snack Mix

Honey Ranch Dip with Veggie Tray

Serve a bowl of your favorite potato chips along with the vegetables.

Dip:
½ cup Mayo
½ cup sour cream
¼ cup buttermilk
3 Tablespoons dry ranch dressing mix
2 Tablespoon honey
1 teaspoon Dijon mustard
1 teaspoon dill weed

Celery sticks
Baby carrots
Green onions
Broccoli and cauliflower cut into flowerets
Cherry tomatoes

Mix all of the ingredients, except veggies, together and place into a serving bowl. Cover and chill. Arrange the veggies on a large platter. Set the dip in the center and serve. Yields 2 cups of dip.

Tip: Add ½ cup buttermilk to make this recipe into a terrific salad dressing.

Sweet and Tangy Meatballs

The meatballs can be made and frozen ahead of time. Simply add the sauce and heat.

Meatballs:
1½ pounds lean ground beef
¼ cup onion, minced
¼ cup green pepper, chopped fine
1 cup fine bread crumbs
1 egg
½ cup ketchup
1 teaspoon garlic salt
1 teaspoon cayenne pepper

Sauce:
1 cup apple or grape jelly
1 cup chili sauce
½ cup honey
1 teaspoon dry mustard

Make the meatballs by mixing all of the ingredients together in a medium mixing bowl until well blended. Make into small meatballs and place onto a baking sheet with sides. Bake at 400 degrees for 20 minutes or until well done. Drain on paper towels. (These can be frozen in an airtight container at this point for up to 2 weeks.) Place the meatballs into a crock-pot. Pour the sauce over the meatballs and heat on low for 2 to 3 hours. Serve hot. Yields 36 small meatballs.

Tip: *This recipe can be easily doubled. Plan on serving 6 meatballs per guest.*

Mini Pigs in Blankets with Honey Mustard Sauce
The honey mustard sauce can be used in countless ways; on sandwiches, as a dip, or as a spread.

1½ pounds cocktail smokies
2 cans crescent rolls, unrolled from the can

Cut each crescent triangle in half. Place a cocktail smokie onto the center of each triangle half. Roll up with the wide edge first. Place on an ungreased baking sheet. Bake at 375 degrees for 8 to 10 minutes. Serve hot with the honey-mustard sauce. Yields 48 appetizers.

Honey Mustard Sauce:
½ cup honey
½ cup yellow mustard
½ cup Mayo
2 Tablespoons Dijon mustard
2 Tablespoons whole grain mustard
1 teaspoon horseradish
1 teaspoon of each of the following: cayenne pepper, garlic salt, curry powder, ginger, dry mustard, and paprika.

Mix all ingredients together in a small mixing bowl. Store in an airtight container or jar. Yields 1½ cups of honey mustard sauce.

Tip: *Make a meat platter by also serving sliced, cooked Brats and Polish sausages or other smoked cooked meats to dip into the honey mustard.*

RECIPES WITH HONEY FOR ALL SEASONS

Honey BBQ Glazed Chicken Wings

Have plenty of napkins on hand for this delicious, easy, spicy sauce.

½ cup honey
½ cup of your favorite BBQ sauce
2 teaspoons Tabasco sauce
1 teaspoon soy sauce
The juice from 1 lemon
Garlic salt
Seasoning salt
Black pepper
Cayenne pepper
4 pounds fresh or frozen then thawed chicken wings

Mix the honey, BBQ sauce, Tabasco sauce, soy sauce and the lemon juice together in a small bowl. Sprinkle the wings with the garlic salt, seasoning salt, black pepper and the cayenne pepper to taste. Bake the wings at 400 degrees for 10 minutes or until lightly for 15 to 20 minutes or until wings are done. Serve hot. Yields about 8 servings.

Tip: *Make these tasty wings into hot wings by adding more cayenne pepper and plenty of Tabasco sauce.*

Honey Caramel Cinnamon Dip with Apples

Kids of all ages love the fall flavors in this dip. Spread it on toast, bagels, or English muffins is for a delicious morning treat.

12 ounces cream cheese, softened
¾ cup brown sugar
¼ cup honey
1 teaspoon cinnamon
1 teaspoon vanilla
Red and Golden Delicious Apple slices

Whip the ingredients, except apples, together with an electric mixer until smooth and creamy. Place in a serving bowl or airtight container and serve with the sliced apples. Yields 1 ½ cups of honey caramel dip.

Tip: Slice the apples into a bowl of chilled ginger ale to keep the apples from turning brown.

Honey Nut Snack Mix

Watch this terrific snack mix quickly disappear, as it has the three ingredients any ball fan will love: popcorn, pretzels, and peanuts.

4 quarts popped corn
2 cups pretzel pieces
2 cups peanuts
1 cup butter
2 cups brown sugar
½ cup honey
2 teaspoons salt
1 Tablespoon vanilla-butter-nut flavoring
½ teaspoon baking soda

Mix the popped corn, pretzels, and nuts together in a large mixing bowl. Mix the butter, brown sugar, honey and salt together in large saucepan. Bring to a boil and lower the heat. Without stirring, slowly boil for 5 minutes. Whisk in the vanilla-nut flavoring and the baking soda quickly. Pour over the popped corn mixture. Using a spoon sprayed with cooking spray, mix the caramel mixture with the popped corn mixture until well coated. Place on 2 greased baking sheets and bake at 250 degrees for 1 hour stirring every 15 minutes. Let the snack mix cool, break up the large pieces and store in an airtight container. Yields 6 quarts of snack mix.

Tip: *Substitute mixed nuts for the peanuts for an even nuttier flavor.*

RECIPES WITH HONEY FOR ALL SEASONS

Chapter 8: Fall

Autumn Harvest

The colors and flavors of fall are painted with broad strokes in this spread fit for a family gathering or company coming for Sunday dinner.

- Corn and Cheddar Appetizer Tarts
- Pear- Pecan- Spinach Salad with Poppy Seed Dressing
- Honey Wheat Knots
- Savory Beef Tips
- Fall Foliage Rice Pilaf
- Pumpkin Spice Trifle

Corn and Cheddar Appetizer Tarts

Start the meal off right with these delectable hors d'oeuvres.
Make these ahead, chill, and cover.
Then bake right before the guests arrive.

Pastry:
1 - 8 ounce package of cream cheese, softened
½ cup butter
1 ½ cups flour
½ cup yellow or white cornmeal
1 teaspoon salt

Filling:
1 cup frozen corn kernels
½ cup green onions, sliced
1 cup cheddar cheese, shredded
4 large eggs, beaten
½ cup cream
1 teaspoon Tabasco Sauce
1 teaspoon Worcestershire Sauce
2 teaspoons honey
Salt and pepper to taste

Mix the pastry ingredients together in an electric mixer until it forms a ball. Roll out into a large circle on a floured surface. Cut with a small cutter and place in mini-muffin tins to form the shells. Sprinkle the corn, green onion and cheese into each mini pastry shell, filling each about half full. Mix the remaining ingredients until smooth. Spoon the egg mixture, (about 1 tablespoon), into each tart until almost full. Bake at 400 degrees for 20 minutes or until the tarts test done by inserting a knife in the center and it comes out clean. Remove from the tins and serve warm. Yields 36 mini tarts.

Tip: *½ cup of bacon can be substituted for the green onion. These are great served with your Thanksgiving dinner.*

Pear Pecan Spinach Salad with Poppy Seed Dressing
The honey-pecans are a sensational snack all by themselves.

6 cups fresh baby spinach leaves, washed and dried
3 large fresh pears, Red or Bartlett
Sugared Pecans
Poppy Seed Dressing

Arrange the spinach on 6 chilled salad plates. Core and slice the pears into chilled ginger ale. Then place a few pear slices attractively on the spinach. Sprinkle about ⅓ cup of the sugared pecans on top of the pear slices. Drizzle desired amount of the poppy seed dressing over the top. Yields 6 servings.

Sugared Pecans:
1 cup of sugar
2 cups of pecan halves

Heat the sugar in a skillet until it just starts to melt, over medium to high heat. Add the pecans and heat and stir until the pecans are well coated and (about 3 to 4 minutes). Place on a greased baking sheet and let cool. Break up the large clusters and store in a zippered plastic bag until ready to serve.

Poppy Seed Dressing:
½ **cup vegetable oil**
¼ **cup honey**
3 Tablespoons orange juice
2 teaspoons poppy seeds
1 teaspoon salt

Shake all ingredients together in a jar with a tight fitting lid until well blended.

Tip: *Apples and almonds may be used in place of the pears and pecans. If serving a large group of guests, place the spinach, pears, and pecans in a large salad bowl. Toss gently and pass the poppy seed dressing around the table.*

Honey Wheat Knots

This versatile dough can be shaped into
rolls, buns, or whole loaves of bread.

1 cup warm water
2 packages of active dry yeast
⅓ cup honey
2 eggs
1 cup warm milk
¼ cup vegetable oil
2 teaspoons salt
3 cups all-purpose flour
3 cups whole wheat flour
½ cup melted butter

Mix the water, yeast, and honey together and let proof until bubbly about 5 minutes. Mix the eggs, warm milk, oil and salt together in a large mixing bowl. Add the yeast mixture. Blend well. Add 1 cup of the all-purpose flour and 1 cup of the whole-wheat flour. Stir until smooth. Add remaining flour, 1 cup at a time until the dough makes a ball. Turn out onto a well-floured surface and knead for 5 minutes, using additional flour until smooth and elastic. Place into a well-greased large bowl and cover with a damp towel. Let rise until doubled. Punch down the dough. Divide the dough into 24 small pieces. Roll each piece of dough into a rope. Dip into the melted butter and tie into a knot shape. Place into 2 well-greased regular-sized muffin tins. Let rise, covered, 15 to 20 minutes or until doubled. Bake at 350 degrees for 20 to 25 minutes or until lightly browned.

Remove from the tins and serve hot. Yields 24 knots.

Tip: *Add 1 teaspoon of garlic and 1 teaspoon of chopped parsley to the melted butter for herbed knots.*

Savory Beef Tips

These tips are so tender they almost melt in your mouth.

2 pounds lean beef sirloin tips, cut into 2-inch pieces

Marinade:
1 cup burgundy wine
¼ cup vegetable oil
2 Tablespoons Worcestershire sauce
1 teaspoon garlic
1 teaspoon parsley
1 teaspoon rosemary
1 teaspoon thyme
¼ cup honey
1 teaspoon sage
1 teaspoon of salt and pepper

Sauce:
1- 10 ¾ can condensed mushroom soup, undiluted
1- 10 ¾ can condensed tomato soup, undiluted
1 package dry onion soup mix
1 package brown gravy mix
1 cup beef broth or burgundy wine
3 tablespoons cornstarch

Mix the marinade ingredients in a large glass or plastic bowl. Add the sirloin tips and toss until well coated. Cover and chill over night for the best results. Drain and discard the marinade. Place the tips into a greased roasting pan. Blend the sauce ingredients together in a mixing bowl.

Then pour over the tips. Bake at 325 degrees for 3 to 4 hours or until the meat is tender and the sauce is thickened. Yields 6 hearty servings.

***Tip:** Cook in a crock-pot on low for 6 hours for simple preparation. This is also delicious served over cooked noodles or garlic mashed potatoes.*

Fall Foliage Rice Pilaf

The colors of autumn come alive in this attractive side dish.

1 cup long-grain white rice
½ cup wild rice
⅓ cup butter
1 cup celery, sliced
1 cup carrots, diced
1 red bell pepper, diced
½ cup yellow onion, chopped
1 teaspoon orange zest
3 teaspoons honey
Salt and pepper to taste
2 cups boiling apple cider

Sauté the long-grain and wild rice in the butter for about 3 minutes or until the white rice is golden. Add the celery, carrots, red bell pepper and onion, Sauté for 5 minutes. Add the orange zest, honey, salt, pepper and the boiling cider. Cover and reduce heat. Simmer for 20 minutes or until cider is absorbed and rice is tender. Yields 6 servings.

Tip: *Garnish with orange slices and parsley sprigs. Chicken broth may be used instead of the cider.*

Pumpkin Spice Trifle
Serve this with a rich, full-bodied coffee or
hot cider for the ultimate fall dessert.

Pumpkin Spice Cake:
1 - 2-layer spice cake mix
4 eggs
¼ cup vegetable oil
½ cup pumpkin puree, canned or fresh
1 - 3 ounce package French Vanilla instant pudding mix
1 cup Hazelnut non-dairy creamer

Filling
Whipped Cream Mixture

Mix the cake ingredients together in a large mixing bowl and mix on medium speed for 3 minutes. Pour into a greased and floured 9 x 13-inch pan. Bake for 35 to 40 minutes or until cake tests done. Let cool and cut into 2-inch cubes. Set aside. Make the filling and assemble the trifle in the following order: ½ of the cake cubes placed in the bottom of a large trifle dish; ½ of the filling; ½ of the whipped cream mixture. Repeat with the remaining cake cubes, filling and whipped cream mixture. Cover with plastic wrap and chill until serving time. Serve with small desert bowls and let each guest serve themselves.

Filling:
1 ½ cups half and half
1- 3 ounce package of French Vanilla instant pudding mix
¼ cup honey

Whip together until smooth and thickened, about 2 minutes.

Whipped Cream Mixture:
2 cups whipping cream
1 tablespoon honey
½ of a 3 ounce package French Vanilla instant pudding mix

Whip ingredients together until the cream forms stiff peaks. Chill the whipped cream covered before assembling the trifle.

Tip: *Make a Pumpkin Spice Cake with Mousse Topping. Keep the cake in the pan and let cool. Make the filling. Then fold the whipped cream mixture into the filling mixture to make the mousse topping. Spread on the cake. Cover and chill until serving time.*

RECIPES WITH HONEY FOR ALL SEASONS

HONEY TIPS

- Store honey at room temperature, never in the refrigerator before adding to recipes.
- Microwave crystallized honey in a microwave safe container stirring every 30 seconds until crystals dissolve.
- Substitute honey in recipes for sugar. Experiment by using honey for ½ of the sugar and adding more if needed.
- Honey is sweeter than sugar or other sweeteners.
- For each cup of honey used in baking, add ½ teaspoon of baking soda.
- Reduce liquid in baking with honey by ¼ of a cup for each cup of honey used.
- Lower the oven temperature when baking with honey to prevent over-browning.
- Easily measure honey by coating the measuring cup or spoon with cooking spray.
- One 12 ounce jar of honey equals = one standard measuring cup.
- Heat honey slightly in the microwave or on the stove, before adding to liquid ingredients in recipes.
- Never scorch honey when heating or melting honey for measuring.
- Honey should not be given to infants under one year of age, but is safe and wholesome for older children and adults.
- Honey is nature's original sweetener.
- Honey used in baked goods reduces crumbling and keeps breads and cakes fresher longer.

ABOUT THE AUTHOR

Standing on a chair with a dishtowel as an apron, author Diana Bricker started cooking at the age of 4. Her love of cooking and experimenting in the kitchen led her to study catering while raising her 3 sons on a ranch on the Wyoming and South Dakota border. For the past 25 years, she has served and catered several events: weddings, church gatherings, and corporate affairs. Her down-to-earth style and homemade recipes, combined with her desire to please the palate of even the hungriest rancher, make her one-of-a-kind! She wants to share her heart and passion of cooking with the world.

Contact Diana: dbricker@mtsbc.org

Printed in Great Britain
by Amazon